DEDICA

This book is in remembrance of my grandmother and Father Esterine Washington and Buck.

It was difficult watching you both go; however, I know you're both in a better place. The motivation I get to pursue my dreams comes from you two watching over our family and me.

We miss you both dearly.
May you Rest In Peace.

-The Williams Family

Why are Affirmations Important

Affirmations are positive statements that can help you to challenge and overcome self-sabotaging and negative thoughts. When you repeat them often, and believe in them, you can start to make positive changes. ... Self-affirmation may also help to mitigate the effects of stress.

I am brave

101 WORDS OF AFFIRMATIONS

BY; AMENIA WILLIAMS B.S

I am strong

I am free

I am beautiful

101 Words Of Affirmations

By Amenia Williams B.S

Cover Designed by Amenia Williams

Cover Created by Jazzy Kitty Publications

Logo Designs by Andre M. Saunders/Jess Zimmerman

Editor: Amenia Williams B.S

© 2021 Amenia Williams B.S

ISBN 978-1-954425-32-3

Library of Congress Control Number: 2021919714

INTRODUCTION

Daily affirmations can change your day, your mood, your way of life. They can also change the way you think and react. The importance of affirmations is something we overlook.

Affirmations give us a sense of "being"; they make us confident and whole. They give us a WIN state of mind, and they help us keep the positive energy in so that our output breeds nothing but positivity. This book was written to do all of those things.

In my darkest times, I prayed, when I hit depression, I spoke into myself, I told myself that I needed to do better and that I had to stop feeling sorry for myself and the way I felt, I HAD TO FIGHT! I never gave up; I stuck it out and made it happen. I was surrounded by bad energy and I knew it was time for a change. When I started to speak positivity into myself and change my surroundings, I was able to give it a lot more. I was more productive; I was more driven and motivated; most of all, I was happy. When you look at this book, I want you to turn the page and feel the same way about yourself EVERY DAY!

Thank you,
SPC AMENIA WILLIAMS

Morning Routine
- Checklist -

Wake up and Thank yourself ○

Make bed ○

Drink water ○

20 min walk, yoga, or jogging ○

Morning journal ○

Take a shower ○

Eat a healthy breakfast ○

Get ready for the day! ♥

7 Day
Gratitude Challenge

01 Journal 3 things you're grateful for

02 Make a list of your accomplishments

03 Celebrate how far you've come

04 Open the door for someone

05 Get your bedroom organized

06 Donate Something

07 Clean out your kitchen cabinets

6 Days
Self-Care Challenge

DAY 1

Clean up your space for 10 minutes.

DAY 2

Embrace forgiveness for a past mistake.

DAY 3

Connect with people who share your beliefs.

DAY 4

Make a positive affirmation related to your goal.

DAY 5

Limit your screen time today, don't check social media.

DAY 6

Learn something new.

Goal Setting The Dr. Williams Way

GOALS

ACTIONS TO TAKE

MOTIVATIONS

STEPS

POTENTIAL PROBLEMS

PROGRESS TRACKER

Set the goals girl!

GOALS	STEPS
	☐
	☐
	☐

POTENTIAL PROBLEMS	
	☐
	☐
	☐

STRATEGIES	
	☐
	☐
	☐

PROGRESS TRACKER	
Date	Progress

Daily affirmation No. 1

I CHOOSE TO BE CALM AND
CONFIDENT ABOUT MY
FUTURE.

Repeat it through the day.

Daily affirmation No. 2

I GROW MORE CONFIDENT
AND STRONGER EACH DAY.

Repeat it through the day.

Daily affirmation No.3

I AM THE ARCHITECT OF MY LIFE. I DESIGN ITS STRUCTURE.

Repeat it through the day.

Daily affirmation No. 4

I BUILD MY LIFE'S FOUNDATION AND CHOOSE ITS CONTENTS.

Repeat it through the day.

FREE YOUR MIND

Daily affirmation No.5

I AM ABOUT TO
SHIFT FROM
WAITING ON IT TO
WALKING INTO IT.

Repeat it through the day.

Daily affirmation No.6

I ACCEPT MYSELF UNCONDITIONALLY.

Repeat it through the day.

Daily affirmation No.7

I RADIATE CONFIDENCE.

Repeat it through the day.

Daily affirmation No.8

I THRIVE ON CHALLENGES THAT BRING OUT THE BEST IN ME.

Daily affirmation No.9

I HAVE CONFIDENCE IN MY ABILITIES AND SKILLS.

Repeat it through the day.

Daily affirmation No.10

I AM BOLD AND
COURAGEOUS.

Repeat it through the day.

NOTES

Self-Care Q&A

ANSWER HONESTLY!

How do I feel today?

_____

What I am thankful for right now?

_____

What negative attitude do I need to change?

_____

What positive affirmation was I able to
give myself today?

_____

What ongoing support do I need?

_____

What do I need to do to be a better version of myself?

_____

Daily affirmation No.11

I AM GUIDED IN MY EVERY
STEP BY SPIRIT WHO LEADS
ME TOWARDS WHAT I MUST
KNOW AND DO.

Repeat it through the day.

Daily affirmation No.12

I AM WORTHY OF HAPPINESS
AND LOVE.

Repeat it through the day.

Daily affirmation No.13

I AM OPTIMISTIC ABOUT THE FUTURE.

Repeat it through the day.

Daily affirmation No.14

I TRUST IN MY ABILITY TO CREATE A FABULOUS FUTURE.

Repeat it through the day.

Daily affirmation No.15

I LET GO OF WORRIES AND REPLACE THEM WITH EXCITEMENT AND OPTIMISM.

Repeat it through the day.

I HAVE ALL IT TAKES TO MAKE MY DREAMS A REALITY.

Repeat it through the day.

Daily affirmation No.17

I AM A KIND AND UNIQUE PERSON WITH A LOT TO OFFER.

Repeat it through the day.

I ENJOY MY OWN COMPANY
AS I GET IN TOUCH WITH MY
TRUE SELF.

Repeat it through the day.

Daily affirmation No.19

I REJUVENATE EVERY PART
OF MY BEING WITH THE HELP
OF SOLITUDE.

Repeat it through the day.

Daily affirmation No.20

I AM AT PEACE AND I AM

HAPPY

Repeat it through the day.

NOTES

Self-Care Q&A

ANSWER HONESTLY!

How do I feel today?

_____

What I am thankful for right now?

_____

What negative attitude do I need to change?

_____

What positive affirmation was I able to
give myself today?

_____

What ongoing support do I need?

_____

What do I need to do to be a better version of myself?

_____

Daily affirmation No. 21

I BRIGHTEN ANOTHER
PERSON'S DAY BY DOING
SOMETHING WITH THEM.

Repeat it through the day.

Daily affirmation No.22

MY INTUITION AND WISDOM GUIDE ME IN THE RIGHT DIRECTION.

Daily affirmation No.23

I AM THE SHIT!

Repeat it through the day.

Daily affirmation No. 24

I HAVE FAITH IN MYSELF TO MAKE THE BEST DECISION POSSIBLE.

Daily affirmation No.25

I HAVE CONFIDENCE IN MY DECISIONS.

Repeat it through the day.

Daily affirmation No.26

REPLACE NEGATIVE CRITICISM WITH ENCOURAGING STATEMENTS.

Repeat it through the day.

Daily affirmation No. 27

I BELIEVE IN MY ABILITY TO OVERCOME SETBACKS.

Repeat it through the day.

EVEN MY "FLAWS" HAVE GOOD AND HELPFUL ASPECTS.

Daily affirmation No.29

I LOVE AND APPROVE OF
MYSELF.

Repeat it through the day.

I TRUST MYSELF TO BE HONEST WITH MYSELF AND OTHERS.

NOTES

Self-Care Q&A
ANSWER HONESTLY!

How do I feel today?

_____

What I am thankful for right now?

_____

What negative attitude do I need to change?

_____

What positive affirmation was I able to
give myself today?

_____

What ongoing support do I need?

_____

What do I need to do to be a better version of myself?

_____

Daily affirmation No.31

I AM AN INSPIRATION TO OTHERS.

Repeat it through the day.

I MATTER AND WHAT I HAVE
TO OFFER ALSO MATTERS.

Daily affirmation No. 33

I TRUST MY INNER WISDOM
AND INTUITION.

Repeat it through the day.

Daily affirmation No.34

WONDERFUL THINGS UNFOLD
BEFORE ME.

Repeat it through the day.

Daily affirmation No.35

I LET GO OF MY ANGER SO I CAN SEE CLEARLY.

Repeat it through the day.

Daily affirmation No. 36

I AM MUCH MORE THAN ADEQUATE; I'M PHENOMENAL!

Repeat it through the day.

Daily affirmation No.37

I GIVE UP THE HABIT OF CRITICIZING MYSELF.

Repeat it through the day.

Daily affirmation No.38

I DEVELOP THE MINDSET TO PRAISE MYSELF.I DEVELOP THE MINDSET TO PRAISE MYSELF.

Repeat it through the day.

Daily affirmation No.39

I AM A GOOD PERSON AT ALL TIMES OF THE DAY AND NIGHT

Repeat it through the day.

Daily affirmation No.40

WHEN I BREATH, I INHALE
CONFIDENCE AND EXHALE
DOUBT.

Repeat it through the day.

NOTES

Self-Care Q&A

ANSWER HONESTLY!

How do I feel today?

_____

What I am thankful for right now?

_____

What negative attitude do I need to change?

_____

What positive affirmation was I able to
give myself today?

_____

What ongoing support do I need?

_____

What do I need to do to be a better version of myself?

_____

Daily affirmation No.41

I DO NOT CARE WHAT OTHER
PEOPLE THINK OF ME. THEIR
OPINION OF ME IS NONE OF
MY BUSINESS

Repeat it through the day.

Daily affirmation No. 42

I AM DESTINED TO BE GREAT,

MY PAST WAS TOO PAINFUL

NOT TO HAVE PURPOSE.

Repeat it through the day.

Daily affirmation No. 43

MY HEART IS ALWAYS OPEN.

Repeat it through the day.

Daily affirmation No.44

I AM SURROUNDED BY LOVE.

Repeat it through the day.

Daily affirmation No.45

LOVE, FORGIVENESS, AND
UNDERSTANDING ARE THE
FOUNDATION OF MY
RELATIONSHIPS.

Repeat it through the day.

Daily affirmation No.46

I AM OUTGOING AND ENRICH OTHER PEOPLE'S LIVES.

Daily affirmation No. 47

THE COMPANY OF STRANGERS TEACHES ME MORE ABOUT MYSELF.

Repeat it through the day.

Daily affirmation No.48

I AM SURROUNDED BY
ABUNDANCE.

Repeat it through the day.

Daily affirmation No.49

I ATTRACT MONEY
EFFORTLESSLY AND EASILY.

Repeat it through the day.

Daily affirmation No.50

I CONTINUOUSLY DISCOVER
NEW AVENUES OF INCOME.

Repeat it through the day.

NOTES

Self-Care Q&A

ANSWER HONESTLY!

How do I feel today?

_____

What I am thankful for right now?

_____

What negative attitude do I need to change?

_____

What positive affirmation was I able to
give myself today?

_____

What ongoing support do I need?

_____

What do I need to do to be a better version of myself?

_____

Daily affirmation No.51

I AM HEALTHY, ENERGETIC, AND OPTIMISTIC.

Repeat it through the day.

Daily affirmation No.52

EVERY DAY I GET HEALTHIER
AND MORE FIT.

Repeat it through the day.

Daily affirmation No.53

MY BODY VIBRATES WITH
ENERGY AND HEALTH.

Repeat it through the day.

I AM COMPLETELY PAIN FREE AND MY BODY IS ENERGIZED.

Daily affirmation No.55

I PAY ATTENTION TO WHAT
MY BODY NEEDS FOR
HEALTH AND VITALITY.

Repeat it through the day.

Daily affirmation No.57

MY BODY, MIND, AND SOUL
WORK TOGETHER
EFFICIENTLY TO KEEP ME
HEALTHY.

Repeat it through the day.

Daily affirmation No.58

I LOVE EVERYTHING ABOUT
MY BODY.

Repeat it through the day.

Daily affirmation No. 5P

I APPRECIATE MY BODY'S UNIQUE TRAITS.

Daily affirmation No.60

I AM THANKFUL FOR THE
SHAPE OF MY BODY.

Repeat it through the day.

NOTES

Self-Care Q&A

ANSWER HONESTLY!

How do I feel today?

_____

What I am thankful for right now?

_____

What negative attitude do I need to change?

_____

What positive affirmation was I able to
give myself today?

_____

What ongoing support do I need?

_____

What do I need to do to be a better version of myself?

_____

MY BODY IS BEAUTIFUL AND APPEALING.

Repeat it through the day.

Daily affirmation No.62

MY BODY IS HEALTHY AND

FULL OF ENERGY.

Repeat it through the day.

Daily affirmation No.63

I AM FILLED WITH
EXCITEMENT WHEN I LOOK
IN THE MIRROR.

Repeat it through the day.

Daily affirmation No.64

I PLAY A BIG ROLE IN MY OWN CAREER SUCCESS.

Repeat it through the day.

Daily affirmation No.65

EVERY CHOICE I MAKE LEADS

TO BIGGER AND BETTER

OPPORTUNITIES.

Daily affirmation No.66

I FIND SOMETHING POSITIVE
ABOUT EVERY SITUATION.

Repeat it through the day.

Daily affirmation No.67

I FIND OPTIMISTIC WAYS OF
DEALING WITH DIFFICULTIES.

Repeat it through the day.

Daily affirmation No.68

I FIND WAYS TO PRAISE OTHERS AND OFFER HELPFUL SUGGESTIONS.

Daily affirmation No.69

TODAY, I MAKE A COMMITMENT TO GIVE OTHERS WHAT I WANT TO RECEIVE.

Repeat it through the day.

Daily affirmation No.70

I USE STRATEGIES THAT MOTIVATE ME TO MOVE FORWARD.

Repeat it through the day.

NOTES

Self-Care Q&A

ANSWER HONESTLY!

How do I feel today?

_____

What I am thankful for right now?

_____

What negative attitude do I need to change?

_____

What positive affirmation was I able to
give myself today?

_____

What ongoing support do I need?

_____

What do I need to do to be a better version of myself?

_____

Daily affirmation No.71

I CHOOSE TO PARTICIPATE
FULLY IN MY DAY.

Repeat it through the day.

Daily affirmation No.72

I TAKE A MINI-BREAK FROM THE PROBLEM TO LET MY SUBCONSCIOUS FIND THE ANSWER.

Repeat it through the day.

Daily affirmation No.73

I BELIEVE IN MY ABILITY TO
FIND AND NAVIGATE THE
PATH THAT'S RIGHT FOR ME.

Repeat it through the day.

Daily affirmation No.74

I RELEASE MY NEED TO HAVE THE APPROVAL OF OTHERS.

Repeat it through the day.

Daily affirmation No.75

I GAIN JOY, FULFILLMENT, AND HAPPINESS FROM THIS DAY.

Repeat it through the day.

Daily affirmation No.76

MY PAST DOES NOT DEFINE
MY FUTURE

Repeat it through the day.

Daily affirmation No.77

TODAY I BURY THE OLD HURT
ME

Daily affirmation No.78

I HAVE ALL IT TAKES TO MAKE THIS DAY PRODUCTIVE.

Repeat it through the day.

I FACE DIFFICULTIES WITH COURAGE AND DETERMINATION.

Repeat it through the day.

Daily affirmation No.80

NEW AND EXCITING OPPORTUNITIES MANIFEST IN MY LIFE CONTINUALLY.

Repeat it through the day.

Self-Care Q&A

ANSWER HONESTLY!

How do I feel today?

_____

What I am thankful for right now?

_____

What negative attitude do I need to change?

_____

What positive affirmation was I able to
give myself today?

_____

What ongoing support do I need?

_____

What do I need to do to be a better version of myself?

_____

I CHOOSE TO FREE MYSELF
FROM ALL NEGATIVITY THAT
HAMPERS MY PROGRESS.

Daily affirmation No.81

I CHOOSE TO FREE MYSELF FROM ALL NEGATIVITY THAT HAMPERS MY PROGRESS.

Repeat it through the day.

Daily affirmation No.82

I AM IN CONTROL OF MY
LIFE.

Repeat it through the day.

Daily affirmation No.83

I BELIEVE IN MY ABILITY TO GAIN VALUABLE INSIGHTS FROM ANY SITUATION.

Repeat it through the day.

Daily affirmation No.84

MY MOST IMPORTANT GOAL IS TO BE AT PEACE, REGARDLESS OF THE SITUATION.

Repeat it through the day.

Daily affirmation No.85

I MAKE A CONSCIOUS CHOICE TO BE HAPPY.

Repeat it through the day.

MY BODY IS RELAXED. MY
MIND IS CALM. MY SOUL IS
AT PEACE.

Daily affirmation No.87

I FEEL JOY AND CONTENTMENT IN THIS MOMENT.

Repeat it through the day.

Daily affirmation No.88

I AWAKEN FEELING HAPPY AND ENTHUSIASTIC ABOUT LIFE.

Repeat it through the day.

Daily affirmation No.89

I CAN TAP INTO A WELLSPRING OF INNER HAPPINESS ANYTIME I WISH.

Repeat it through the day.

Daily affirmation No.90

I INSPIRE MYSELF AND
OTHERS TO BE HAPPY BY
MODELING HOW TO DO IT.

Repeat it through the day.

NOTES

Self-Care Q&A

ANSWER HONESTLY!

How do I feel today?

_____

What I am thankful for right now?

_____

What negative attitude do I need to change?

_____

What positive affirmation was I able to
give myself today?

_____

What ongoing support do I need?

_____

What do I need to do to be a better version of myself?

_____

Daily affirmation No.91

I HAVE FUN IN ALL OF MY
ENDEAVORS, EVEN THE
MOST MUNDANE.

Repeat it through the day.

Daily affirmation No.92

I FIND JOY AND PLEASURE IN
THE SIMPLE THINGS OF LIFE.

Repeat it through the day.

Daily affirmation No.93

I REST PEACEFULLY AND SOUNDLY, KNOWING ALL IS WELL IN MY WORLD.

Repeat it through the day.

Daily affirmation No.94

I AM BRIMMING WITH
ENERGY THAT LIFTS MY
SPIRITS THROUGHOUT THE
DAY.

Daily affirmation No.95

MY HEART IS OVERFLOWING
WITH JOY.

Repeat it through the day.

Daily affirmation No.96

I HAVE AN ACTIVE SENSE OF
HUMOR AND LOVE TO LAUGH
WITH OTHERS.

Repeat it through the day.

Daily affirmation No.97

I RELEASE THE PAST AND LIVE FULLY IN THE PRESENT MOMENT.

Repeat it through the day.

Daily affirmation No.98

I MEDITATE EASILY WITHOUT RESISTANCE OR ANXIETY.

Daily affirmation No.99

I AM FREE FROM
DEPRESSION

Repeat it through the day.

MANY PEOPLE LOOK UP TO
ME AND RECOGNIZE MY
WORTH; I AM ADMIRED.

Daily affirmation No.101

I AM A POWERHOUSE; I AM
INDESTRUCTIBLE.

Repeat it through the day.

NOTES

Self-Care Q&A

ANSWER HONESTLY!

How do I feel today?

_____

What I am thankful for right now?

_____

What negative attitude do I need to change?

_____

What positive affirmation was I able to
give myself today?

_____

What ongoing support do I need?

_____

What do I need to do to be a better version of myself?

_____

ABOUT THE AUTHOR

AMENIA WILLIAMS

Amenia was born and raised in Wilmington, DE. She attended Howard High School of Technology and later went on to earn her college degree at Wilmington University.

Amenia is currently pursuing her graduate degrees so that she can one day open up her practice and serve her community. Amenia is now on the road to starting her non-profit organization for at-risk youth.